TRACKINGS

TRACKINGS
The Body's Memory, The Heart's Fiction

9-18-98

*For Yolanta —
with all best
wishes.*

Bill

Bill
Morgan

Dead Metaphor Press
1998

© 1998 BY BILL MORGAN

FIRST EDITION

ISBN 1-880743-08-6

TRACKINGS:
THE BODY'S MEMORY, THE HEART'S FICTION
WAS THE 1996 DEAD METAPHOR PRESS
CHAPBOOK CONTEST WINNER

ACKNOWLEDGEMENTS
POEMS THAT THUMP IN THE DARK MAGAZINE,
POETRY MOTEL, CQ, SOW'S EAR POETRY REVIEW

COVER ARTWORK BY
NICOLAS AFRICANO

AUTHOR PHOTO BY
DEBORAH MOORE

DESIGNED AND EDITED BY
RICHARD WILMARTH

DEAD METAPHOR BOOKS ARE DISTRIBUTED BY
SMALL PRESS DISTRIBUTION AND BY THE PUBLISHER

FURTHER INQUIRIES AND ORDERS
SHOULD BE ADDRESSED TO
DEAD METAPHOR PRESS
P.O. BOX 2076
BOULDER, CO 80306
1-303-417-9398

INCLUDE $1.25 FOR POSTAGE
WHEN ORDERING ONE BOOK
AND $1.75 WHEN ORDERING TWO
OR MORE FROM THE PUBLISHER

Contents

Sounding the Habit of Irony	1
Offerings: November 22	2
Counter Offer	3
Returns: January 12	4
Multiple Choice	5
Bodies: the Spirit Within	7
Self Portrait: Nature Film	8
Ice Storm	9
Saying it Plain	10
Carnal Knowledge	12
Distance and Destinations: April 10	14
At the First Place	15
Falling	17
The One Word	18
Ending: August 10	20
Hide and Seek	21
Of Mourning and Onward Motion	23

Sounding the Habit of Irony

Your sharp, fresh words lying
over beds of loss, shortfall,
rhythms like old desire
patched up and sent back in,
inflections like tiny band-aids
tight over discontinuities,
syntax like scar tissue
built up layer on layer,
sediment of lost languages,
histories, selves—gone,
hidden from me, maybe
from you, but in this room
as geology sits inside time,
as biography floods any now.

Offerings: November 22

When she handed me her poems, I remembered seeing the look before; it had masked something not given when we read Yeats in class, and it flickered across her face again a few minutes later that afternoon in the office, as she watched her daughter, ignoring our talk, walk over and climb, trusting, into my lap.

                      My son saw it too, when, leaving the office just as he arrived (and nearly running him down), she drilled a hole through him with her challenging eyes.

      Who was that? Was she angry?

                                          No, not angry—defiant, I think. She has just now asked me to read her poems.

Counter Offer

Your words lay bare your bruises, leave
you lying open, challenging my care
by claiming you are broken, I am whole;
standing apart, we cannot stand together,

        you would say.

            I deny that.

My counter offer is that we engage
this issue straight ahead—earthlings together:
neither one gets any points for hardship;
neither claims a clearer, cleaner life.

           Agreed?

           If so,

you, you lovely proud fierce wounded woman—
hear this: my loves are feelings bearing choice;
these bodies are for healing souls; when love
moves through the body, wholeness visits earth.

You with your beauty brains passion stand
centered, worthy this world, blood kin with all
I love; I thank you for your courage trust
and give this back. Meet me here; words serve

for now. Standing myself, my body clothed,
I cannot love you naked on your back.

Returns: January 12

A year ago I thought she was gone,
but she came back again: something is still
at stake between us. She said she didn't think
I'd take her seriously. I said it's all I've ever done.
We talked that way for nearly four hours,
and an amazing woman slipped in and replaced
the frightened girl who kept coming back.
Slowly, I felt myself becoming a lover again,
resisting it, wanting it to be true.

It's very late; shall we go to the other room?
I said, laying my hand on hers.
Yes. Scared? Yes. Me too.

Multiple Choice

No script for this—
we'll have to make it up.

Imagine this:
married, babies,
the labor of loving,
claiming history
we didn't live,
me sick at 60,
dead at 70,
you out of time.

Or imagine this:
our class-mates' scorn,
guilty envy—
middle-aged prof,
sweet young thing—
the talk, malice,
public space
like lead boots
to drag us down.

Or this: We quit,
right now, end—
obsession broken,
trophies on the wall.

Try this: You write,
find love, have babies;

I'll write, love the kids
I've got, trust time
and desire. When plots
converge, when character,
argument, design,
rhetoric, form,
politics align
(next week, month,
year), we'll come
together again,

each time, first time,
chosen over and over.

Bodies: the Spirit Within

We embrace, and her face burrows
into the notch of my neck and cheek
like a small animal coming to rest.
Her hands tighten on my shoulders,
speaking plainly: trust, desire—
or drift across my face, or trace
the line of my thigh, like the hands
of the blind, inquiring, memorizing
a new terrain—drawing all of me,
tender, open, out to the skin;
repose follows me up the scale
of pleasure and back; deep rest
nestles within the strenuous—
tingling, claiming me all the way
out to the fingernails:

This is the place where nothing
can be argued, nothing
need be proven; this is
the land of the self-evident.

I had forgotten.

Self Portrait: Nature Film

Out of the quiet cave,
blinking in the light,
yawning, sniffing the air
licking his lips,
testing his limbs,
idly rubbing his butt
on a nearby tree—
rested, curious,
content

until the first
taste of berries

pulls him lurching
happily ahead, nose down,
snuffling in deep
fresh grass, flanks
caressed, combed
by early-season
brush and briars—
tracking the body's memory,
following the bright river.

Ice Storm

Lines down, trees tensed
against the danger, deep-
night shrieks of branches
overweighted, stripped away.

In here, we reached out, finding
each other's limbs, pressing
a human claim, coming together
under covers, pushing back
against all that outside.

Later, lying quiet, safe
against each other, we saw
the bedroom lamp glowing
and heard the furnace purr:
"We did that—right?" "Yeah."
Smiling then, we turned
and slept, fond frail things,
hands still touching—for now
warm, whole again.

Saying it Plain

Saying those words
straight out, plain,
is like courting a friendly
familiar delusion,
like pretending
Lake Michigan salmon
are clean, unspotted.

They're wondrously
beautiful—the length
of their flashing sides,
their power in motion;
but the half-life
of what they bear
within is twice
our term on earth.
So many generations
have pissed in the common
canteen, the sediment
so insinuates itself
along the food chain,
suspending its poisons
up, down the waters,
that being plain
is choosing deadly
immersion, or making
a desperate claim
to a pure grounding
beyond history.

So I want to say it,
yes, but in a hard way:
I do—yes; I love you.
And, despite the damage
done in their name,
I would wish these words
to leap with solid
muscular grace
from the deep gravity
of dying waters,
and claim the sunlight,

refuse to submit
without assertion,

and decline to say
their arc can stand
high, clean in air,
indifferent
to the slide
of waves below.

Carnal Knowledge

The surgeon's knife has been at us both—
claiming me long down the belly,
jogging right
around the navel,
lifting to make an isolated cut
on the left where the colostomy
hung for a while;
marking you in rows I haven't seen
across your back, again on the buttocks
and down the arm (I know this much)—
invading, repairing, restoring.

You were attacked from without—
a terrible scream of speeding metal
(I know this much too)—they lifted
away the skin of your back
to save a peeled left arm;
I from within—a part of me
tried to die and nearly poisoned the rest.

But someone skillful
visited our bodies with instruments,
and left us alive
with a make-do wholeness—
flesh stretched open, drawn tight again
in articulate lines, zones of pink:
"Careful; I was broken here."

When we open to each other,
my history is written plain—
here, run your finger down the line
and read; yours, though, is behind, as if
irrelevant: know me frontally—now;
forget the rest, you seem to say, deftly
removing your shirt and lying back in the dark.

I comply, tender, happy as a child—
hands, lips, chest touching you—carnal
without knowledge,
                        trying to know
the body unmarked, to touch the beauty
of wholeness—like your perfect belly—
but finding only transcendence, landing
again somewhere outside, where history,
the only witness, falls silent.

I crave love's anchor, the particular:
Come, turn around; let me touch your scars
and read. I know their language already.

Distance and Destinations: April 10

All month, arbitrary absence, long-distance talks—tedious, hollow narrative. Then this afternoon, panic over the wires:

You keep on making the impossible possible—
but I've always imagined marriage, a father for
my child, more children: so what am I doing
loving you—long divorced, settled, grown kids?
I'm confused and afraid. I've never been this
happy, but I don't know myself now; I don't
understand these feelings.
                        Nor I. But I
understand mine: I'm a child alone in the dark
woods. I think this was your first exit line.

At The First Place

Each step closer,
I have loved you better:
the year of waiting sharpened
you to a needle's point,
then one winter night set aside
the manic energy, armored
language—removed the last
sliver of air between our chests,
and left us shivering, exposed.

That was layers ago. This week,
the arrowy beauty of now
and the fear of tomorrow's lance
left one more shield lying useless
on the floor and you in doubt
and tears—both of us shaken
again, open as flowers,
staring at our choice.

I will help you put
your clothes back on,
if it's clothing you want,
but listen: for me, this all
hangs together: I take back
none of it, and nothing
we started, nothing we want
feels out of reach: barer
has, each time before,
been better, so why not now?

Whatever follows from this,
whatever becomes us
now has already begun
at the first place
our bodies uncovered.

My measure of then, now,
and later is that trusting
play, kindly passion,
the touch of breath
on skin—is knowing you
tender and bare there
inside.

Falling

It's a children's game—you know it I bet:
you fold your arms across your chest,
close your eyes and let go—falling
backward, blind and reckless, towards
the earth, burying the fear of betrayal
beneath a sure belief in the rules,
the simple trust the other is there—
because that's the agreement.

I remember summer evenings outside
after dark, falling and catching
again and again, domesticating
fear, learning I could choose to fall
without choosing to break my neck.

Yes, I see the glass and rocks
and I know I'm heavy and I remember
when my cousin thought it was funny
to trick me and I know you maybe
don't have the shoulder strength—

but it's too late: my eyes are closed
and I've already leaned beyond
the reasonable limit of gravity,
bulk, and balance—so step behind
and catch or let me fall and learn.

The One Word

> I would like to give you the silver
> branch, the small white flower, the one
> word that will protect you
> from the grief at the center
> of your dream....
>
> —Margaret Atwood

Your sorrow has entered me
like an arrow. I watch
you twist in fear, explode
in rage; I listen to your stories—
I understand, I understand—
from over here, this side
of the line. My own pain,
an echo of yours—older,
subtler, but the same—
has linked me to you.

Take me to the place
where it hurts the most.
I'm not afraid. You won't
die, and I won't flinch
or pull away, when that deepest
wound lies open. I will dare
to say it: You are safe with me—
tell me I'm safe with you.

In simple human love
I want to give you comfort,
healing. But I'm no saint
or martyr—this is mine too,
now; loving you has opened
my oldest hurts.

If we could walk to that place
together, then maybe I could watch
you walk away, or believe you
coming back to a bond
the world can't break:
a connection so rooted
in a knowledge of loss
that love is the only choice,
so accountable to pain
that joy looks rational,
so grounded in betrayal
that faith is all that's left
unknown—out there to be
claimed and earned.

Ending: August 10

Language, the tyrant-artificer of the heart's
fiction, brings me back to *We* even now,
when the woman is gone, her voice fading,
and mine still incanting loss, recovery, loss. . . .

We were afraid, and we made a fearful bargain—
that even if we couldn't live this through,
we'd meet once more, after the last word
was said, with all the armor off.
                                It came
all at once: hot tears, a fierce embrace,
and then: I'm sorry—I can't. . . . An hour
later, alive in our skins alone: Are you sure
you don't want to do this again?
                                      I was just
thinking the same thing.
                        Next day, she went away
determined, both of us cracked into shards.

Hide and Seek

You have been having a love affair
with impossibility, not with me—
or with the others. You've been hiding,
and I, brandishing the claim
of the possible, have been It.

Every place you've hidden before,
I've found you and called you out
with careful, thoughtful love:
"No; not impossible—only difficult."
But now you've gone again, this time
to the last hiding place, the one
you know I could never enter as myself;
you've slipped behind a guarded ring
of fire, and through the flames you say,
This is now my world:
here at least my anger's justified;
my Mother says I'll burn in hell—
her injustice makes my rancor just;
oppression, cruelty tell me who I am;
here laughter has the bitter edge I like—
the outlaw's caustic, cynical repose,
the victim's deep, ironic resonance;
put on the asbestos armor, and come,
find and love me, friend, while I
love these, my guards.
                    No; too late
for that. The armor doesn't fit
me now; you taught me to like going

without.
      You had a good head start
from those who battered you all your life,
but you have chosen this destination
for yourself. I'm angry at you for hiding
there; no love of mine can take
me where you are.
                    You win. I quit
being It.

If you grow tired or afraid, come out
some night, stand still in the light,
and look this way—call my name
when the possible warms your veins again.
I will hear you. You won't have to search.
For all the midnight runs I've made
into the fearsome lands you travel in—
for all the anger, the weariness—
my home address is still the same;
if you want me whole, proposing the possible,
come back; I can't come to you this time.

Of Mourning and Onward Motion

> —I haven't met that many happy people in my life;
> How do they act?
>
> —The Big Chill

This has been a failure
of imagination,
not courage.
I can see that now.

My Multiple Choice, for instance,
didn't foresee this one:
violation, denial, abandonment—
great treble hooks sunk
in each other's wounds
like pike lures wedged in moss—
slowly drawing out chunks
on a strong, slender fiber
of longing and need.

Looking just ahead,
you saw teeth, knives,
panic, cries for help
you didn't dare answer—
so you cut the line.

I saw lovers,
just escaping
explosion and shipwreck,

outside looking back
at all that loss—seared,
drenched—
        whispering
"Look, we have come through!"

embracing,
        then turning to search
for survivors.

In my version, back on shore,
we were two mere mortals
no longer needing to trust ourselves
alone but riding the onward movement
of the earth—borne along
like children, fuller, more able
with each revolution,
each walk around the block.

Your Obsession, too,
yearned for shared innocence,
but named it as something
given, not achieved—already
out there—like a lost beginning,
an invisible treasure, waiting
to be claimed.

So no—I had you wrong—
you'd want to skip the embrace,
face disaster and head
for the wreck; of course.
And you had me wrong too,

since I'd want to pause and look
at the amazing privilege—part given
part earned—of shared survival,
then earn it by handing it back.

The whole time, wherever you looked,
you saw an oak and a stick; and I saw
two fond, frail humans who might
get lucky, then learn to deserve it.
We both were wrong.

Last night as I walked the dog
around the block, a young woman—
younger than you—leaned out
the window of a passing car
and shot me—her lips pursing just
enough for the silent pow—
with a late-August zucchini
(you know the kind—big,
seed-heavy), and I smiled, puzzled,
thinking you probably would understand
and wondering if that was what
you had meant to do.

But for living, wonder won't do.
So it's not surprising that, after
I've cooked and done the dishes
tonight, I'm walking the dog again—
or that, a long way back in our history,
imagination quietly seduced the literal:
I meant it all, beloved—both ways,
all the way through.

25

Bill Morgan, a native of Atlanta, Georgia, teaches in the English department at Illinois State University. He writes, fishes, and tries to live thoughtfully in Normal, Illinois with his partner, Deborah and their ancient cat, Tosca.

This edition
was published
in an
edition of
250 copies,
10 of
which were
numbered and
signed by the author
and cover artist, Nicolas Africano

Trackings
was also
published
in a
special
edition of
100 copies,
10 of
which were
numbered and
signed by the author
and cover artist, Ann Ellis

Both editions
are listed separately
in *Books in Print*

Dead Metaphor Press Booklist

Ten Degrees Cooler Inside
Poetry by Aimée Grunberger. $4.95

8-Ball
Poetry by Jack Collom
w/Illustrations by
Donald Guravich. $7.95

Voices in the Room
Poetry by Richard Wilmarth. $4.95

West Is Left on the Map
Poetry by Anselm Hollo
w/Illustrations by
Jane Dalrymple-Hollo. $4.95

Journal of the Lingering Fall
Poetry/Prose by Tree Bernstein. $4.95

The Henry Miller Acrostics
Poetry by Richard Wilmarth. $5.95

First Love and Others
Prose by Tracy Davis $4.95